From ZERO to HERO

HOSPITALITY SECRETS

Linda Zambrano Dachova
www.worldoflinda.sk

How to become a hospitality professional

Become a hospitality professional, make more money .
About how to be the best on what you do.
Informations for all involved - employees, owners and curious people

Author: Linda Zambrano Dachova

Hello, My name is Linda and my specialization is customer service and hospitality. I believe this eBook will help you along the way in your professionalism and after reading you will be closer to your goals.

STATEMENT:

This material is an information product. Any use or copying of the text of this work without the author's permission is a violation of copyright law and may be prosecuted. The photos were used from the public unsplash site. The opinions and recommendations of third parties are also used in this product. This information is only a recommendation and expression of the author's personal opinion on the subject. Success is up to you and the author is not responsible for any failures.

Thank you for reading this words…….

I was guided by the idea to help you better understand what hospitality is , what you need to know and what is required.
 This is a informations about worldwide services, no matter where you are. It's about how you can get the most out of your work to the satisfaction of both your client and yours. You will find many practical and instructive examples of life in the hospitality. The eBook is designed for those interested in improving service quality, and will also help business owners and service managers who can train "their" people and lead to success and curious people to expand their insight.

After 25 years of working in hospitality home and abroad, I consider this to be a dream job. Why? It is exclusive, very well paid and has helped me fulfill all my desires. This job taught me patience, listening to clients and responding quickly to different situations. I am grateful that I had the opportunity to travel, earn and learn. I fulfill my work and personal goals, and it pushes me forward. As a human, professional, student. I understand that education is a lifetime process, and the opportunity to sell your experience to others and see their success is the best motivation for further work.

Wish you a pleasant reading…..

In case you will have a questions, remarks or referencies please write me on linda@worldoflinda.sk

CONTENT:

1. Hospitality industry…………………………………………..8

2. Restaurant – effective performance…………………..20

3. Learn, learn and learn………………………………………...28

4. Customer needs……………………………………………….35

5. Know your client………………………………………………...39

6. How to exchange a feeling for more money………….42

7. Success will come – just keep going…………………….46

8. Cruise ships – best hospitality……………………………..48

9. Stories for inspiration………………………………………...62

From Zero to Hero – it's like a fairy tale how John became a king. The poor and honest boy became a king because he won the battle with the dragon and saved the princess. Nowadays, this means to fight the obstacles and challenges you have in business. In this book, you will develop techniques and understands how to become the HERO. In your business, in what will keep you going every day. In what you will enjoy and will bring you success.

It all starts with a dream. I dream about what I want and what I long for. Working in the hospitality is difficult but will always bring sweet fruit. No need to worry about . Even if you haven't worked in the hospitality, it's never too late to get started. However, one thing to remember:

"The customer is the most important visitor in our premises. He is not dependent on us, we are dependent on him. It is not an interruption of our work, it is its purpose. He is not an outsider of our business; We do not do him a favor by serving him, He does us a favor by giving us an opportunity. "- Mahatma Gandhi, the greatest servant of mankind of the century

If you **follow** this rule, you **succeed.** It doesn't matter which **direction** you go - success is **guaranteed**. Great Mahatma Gandhi was a servant all his life. You **need** to have kindness and modesty and success is with you. Clients like to **return** to places where they felt **good** and was well taken **care** of.

And that is what is the **pillars** of today's modern age. Service, pleasant environment, **understanding** people. Business services have **changed** a lot over the last 20 years. For better. Anyone could work in **hospitality** today. The industry has changed and needs more

professionals . However, they were not born, they **learned** and practiced to get where they **are** today.

Years ago, **wages** in hospitality were minimal, but **today** they are **different**. There is more to earn in **hospitality** than in other industries. You just need to know **how** to do it. Today, customers pay extra for willingness and good **service**. With pleasure!

The new generation is already **focused** on the **quality** and value they receive in **exchange** for their money. They live a consumer life, indulges in everything that is **possible** and establishes the family at a higher age than 30 years ago. Therefore, is more educated, experienced travellers and more **demanding**. They are not afraid to say their **opinion** - and loudly - and **always** expects more. Today's "Millennium Generation" is computer-oriented, visiting sites **based** on recommendations, and watching "influencers" - people which all **follows** and they set the tone not only in fashion but **overall** lifestyle.

They **write** reviews and ratings and **share** them with everyone they know and do not know. And today on this **your** business stands or falls. It just depends on **how** quickly you adapt to trends and learn to sense the needs of your **customers**. Your entire business is **based** on your **attitude**. You can earn more on your **approach** and lead by example. An **example** to your colleagues, employees, competitors.

Change your approach and your **income** will change as well. Income of informations, finances and pleasure in life. You need to understand the **basic** simple principle of doing **business** and you have it. Success comes. And it does not matter age, sex, color or past. **Everyone** can be the **Hero**. It's up to you.

There is a **lot** of literature, training courses, but the **goal** is always the same. Offer **quality**, skills, experience, professionalism and create an **impression**. The main concern is customer **satisfaction** and his return to **your** business.

Always be a step ahead and use **all** available means to get the best **result.** Follow best practices and **educate** yourself.
This is the golden key.

1. HOSPITALITY INDUSTRY

The service area **includes** not only catering - restaurants, hotels, cafeés and bars, fast food and restaurant departments in shopping centers.

However, it includes **all services**, taxi, exchange offices, banks, bicycle rent, car rental, massage, relax and fitness centers, water parks, campings, museums, hairdressers and pedicures... just everything where you pay **attention** to your **customers**. The number of family-run accommodation and professional rental apartments is also on the rise. And where is a **service** , there are **customers**. And where is a **good** service , there is also a good **money**.

When you are just starting out or have already run a business, have been doing your job for years or days, it is **always** a good idea to **follow** new trends, industry **developments**.
We have classic hotels, floating hotels, cottages and apartments for rent and various restaurants. But there is one **rule** everywhere - the **customer** is always right.

HOTELS:

There are many kinds of **hotels**. From the small, privately owned or family owned to the large famous multinational chains . However, they have one thing in common - they offer **comfort** and fight the competition.

Work at the hotel is **beautiful**. There are many opportunities. From **welcoming** staff, luggage carriers, messengers, reception, hotel and restaurant to relaxation center. In **every** place we offer our **clients** quality, comfort and **experience**.

Clients come here with their families, relatives, people they love and want to **enjoy** the best - relax without worrying and spend as much time together as possible. From the entrance to the hotel they want to **feel welcome**, pampered, **attended** .

It is **important** to focus on customers from the very **firs**t moment. With a **smile** everything goes **better**. Smiling porter, receptionist, lift service. This is the **base** for **success**. Yes - a smile. At job interviews, HR officers choose people who are **positively** tuned and **smiling**.

Imagine the situation - you bought a weekend to surprise your wife. You look forward to it for last 3 months. With workload and constant travel, you will finally relax. You park your car in front of the hotel. You're going in ... nobody anywhere.

On the counter you will see a bell and it says "When you are already here - ring the bell"

You will ring and wait. After a while, the lady in middle age comes in, has towels over her shoulders and begins to explain that her job is also to make a laundry, so goes straight from there.

She asks for your reservation (you need to find the whole e-mail on your phone) and then hands you the key and two towels straight from her shoulder, explaining that it's outside in the second building through the parking lot to the left. Instructions for accommodation are in the room. You look at each other and slowly disappear into place.

First, you look at the way to the room - fortunately, the luggage can easily be moved from the car and it's on the ground floor. You open the room and you are immediately see a large board. You have everything on it. From the restaurant, a sauna, a parking lot, and a notice of when to leave the room on the day of departure. You've also found a wi-fi password so the weekend can begin - by reading the instructions

Now imagine the second situation. The door opens to you automatic , inside you are greeted by gentleman with a trolley and he offers you a luggage transport - whether by yourself or with his help. The receptionist welcomes you with the words "Welcome I believe you will feel comfortable with us." He only asks for your surname, explains everything from a restaurant to a city tour and wishes you a pleasant stay.

Do you see the **difference**? Ordinary stay for two days. For the **same** price. In the **same** town. Tested. Own experience. You are fine - but if you will look for a weekend for two again or need to recommend this in the future, **for sure** you are going to hotel number 2.

In this direction we **must** think and every day. That's the difference - a **SMILE**.

RECEPTION DESK

Reception desk can be **anywhere**. In the hotel, in the beauty center, in the water park, in the fitness center. The work there is not **easy**, but can be **managed**. To work at the reception desk, it is **necessary** to have the computer skills at an advanced level, know the spelling and writing, **communicate** with clients and employees, and the bonus is when the receptionist speaks **at least** one foreign language. First of all, it is necessary to learn what is most **needed**. When you need to search something **quickly** in the database you will be **ready** only if you **know** the system. Pay attention every day when you have the **time** - at the beginning or end of a work shift, what you actually do and what you can **learn**. You certainly **know** the basic functions of the programs used, but try something **new**.

Friendliness is **natural** need and professionalism as well. Always be a step ahead of the client and **learn** telephone ethics. Introduce your company name and yourself when answering a call, **make sure** to add "what can I do for you?" or "How may I assist you?"

The work at the reception desk is **different**. From own **communication** with clients to handling orders, reservations, **planning** of cleaning work. It all depends on the size and structure of the **organization**. In some hotels, the reception is **also** responsible for ordering laundry, making restaurant materials orders and others. In the small fitness receptionist is **responsible** for the cleanliness of all the spaces etc.

If the facility **has** an operational manager, is usually his **responsibility**. 25 years ago it was common that when there was a lot of work in the restaurant, the receptionist was **helping** in the restaurant, the housekeeping ladies **helped** to wash the plates in the kitchen, etc.

Today, **most** of employees has their **designated** function and public health cerificate. They only does what they **have to** do and what he was **assigned** for. Is good to **find out** if professional growth and feature changes are needed. Let executives also **focus** on the quality of their employees and colleagues.

Practical example – 20 years ago new waitress was hired. In the restaurant was fast, organized, guests liked her. By conversation and observation, her supervisor discovered that she has a computer skills, studied foreign languages and hotel is missing receptionist at this moment. She was invited to a short interview. Management explained the expectations and the girl confirmed that she could handle it. Other waiter was hire, she took offered position. Today she is a hotel manager - for last 15 years

Do not be **afraid** to change employees, **assign** them to other functions. Everyone has **different** abilities and skills. The sooner you figure it out, the **sooner** your business or work will **succeed**. Employees can also be **motivated**. Longtime fitness receptionist has **certified** her skills and today she is the **professional** trainer.

When you **selecting** your employees it is important to think about the **future** needs. Same when employee is **accepting** the job you have to make a **plan**. Make your **goals** for the next month, half a year, one year. **Write** your short-term and long-term goals into a visual form - board and watch it **every** day.

Plan **ahead**. If you know you **need** reinforcements for the season, start **recruiting** a few months in **advance**. Ask friends for recommendations and **look** for potential - specialized schools, hobby clubs.

Have a **discussion** with your team. About what and how to **improve**, **listen** the comments and use all the **feedback** they give you. If someone is **interested** in reassigning, think about it. Also, if you are thinking of working in a **different** position as an employee, **express** yourself.

When you have a hotel you **need** a restaurant. Whether it will **offer** services only to hotel guests or random **customers** is up to the management.
It is good to **offer** at least breakfast, even if the hotel is small. Your **guests** will appreciate it.

It does not have to be a big one - you can serve a **cold** breakfast made of simple food or even vacuum **packages**. If you have a capacity, **hot** breakfast will be appreciated.

I have also experienced a case where 5 small family hotels used a nearby restaurant to offer a food to their clients. Each hotel had 2 apartments, an average of 4 people a day. In the season with children it was even more. So the restaurant had at least 20 guests for breakfast every day. Good, isn't it?

Salaries can vary depending on the country, location and nature of the venues.

In Slovakia **approximate** earnings are as follows: / SOURCE - PAYMENTS. SK /, where the amount of wages may be **different** from regions and wages are gross:

Chambermaid 720 EUR

Executive chef 1427 EUR

Sous chef 920 EUR

Assistant chef 760 EUR

Dish wash cleaner 655 EUR

Restaurant manger 1147 EUR

Bartender 782 EUR

Receptionist 786 EUR

General Manager 1156 EUR

PRIVATE APARTMENTS, ROOMS, CHALETS FOR RENT:

Apartment or house for rent is also an **opportunity** to work in **hospitality**. If you have an unused cottage or a grandparent's house, you can use it to get **extra** income, or make a main **business** from it.

I know people who work abroad and all their time spend outside the country they are renting their apartment. Not all, only one room out of three but still brings them around 350 euros a month, where 100 is giving the lady for a cleaning after the weekends.

They do this only occasionally so that they have extra money to pay the rent and energy. However, I know another professional who has 4 appartments and receives approximately 2400 EUR a month all year if he only has only3 days a week occupied.
However, he cleans himself and involves his adult children in this process also.

If you have **apartments** for rent and guests take **turns** every 3 days, **communication** is the **most** important. The best is to contact the client as **soon** as they arrive, can be **done** by phone. **Always** make sure it is personal. **Adress** the client by his **name** and ask the **questions**. Today it common that you **offer** a free map of the surrounding area and **give** a good tips where to go and what to experience. This **effort** will surely **return** to you in the form of references and **increased** number of **new** clients.

When you **offering** a rent of flats or rooms through **internet** portals you can have **income** from 15 to 1500 EUR per person per night. It all **depends** on your options and client **interest**. Offer something 'extra' and you'll be sold out for the **whole** season. It doesn't have to be a lot - offer a city **tour**, theater **tickets** or a water park tickets. If you **offer** a free tourist map with public transportation options and **provide** an electronic rechargeable **chip** (which clients will return to you on departure), you have **everything** on your side.

Make **sure** your place **always** shines **clean**. Unwashed stairs or windows will be the **first** thing the client notices when entering. The furnishings of the apartment and the rooms are better **simple**, easy to maintain and **clean.** Ventilation, whether natural or air-conditioned, should always be fresh so that the client does not "get a bad breeze" when the door is opened.

Automatic key code door system is great. Invest in this technology, it pays off. **Browse** pages and reviews of similar devices on your neighborhood and **learn**. Copy what is **good** and **improve** what is not. Full equipped kitchen, wi-fi, washing machine ... this is a standard now . **Quality** beds, interestning upholstery fabrics and well designed spaces will do the best.

Have your business officially **legalized**. Because even the neighbor who lives next to you for 40 years can **talk** about your accommodation somewhere. And the cousin who works in the tax office **might** look at you and **you** have a problem.

HAIRDRESSERS, MANICURES, MASSAGE CENTERS

These facilities have **specific** rules. Mostly they are operated by one person and by agreement the groups work together. They have one or no reception. They offer services **individually** and are interested in building a stable base of **customers**.

They more easily **implement** all the principles of customer service because the **quality** of their service is directly related to earnings. It has long been true that the better the **service,** the better the reward.

2. RESTAURANT - EFFECTIVE PERFORMANCE

Restaurants can **be found** almost everywhere. They are differently divided, categorized and offer **different** kinds of food and drinks. Waiters, cooks, bartenders, sommeliers and all **involved** form one **team**. They must work **together** for satisfaction of their **customers**.

Everyone has a role and **together** they are a **TEAM**. In this work the base is **communication**. With the client and with each other. Waiters - they are an important part, they are **representatives** of the **whole** company. Not only for themselfs, but also for all cooks, utilities workers, **the owner.**

A restaurant worker **should** have a certain **standard**. Be nicely groomed, in clean clothes, scented. Not too much, just nice. There's nothing worse than having a waiter bend over and his aromatic armpits will be the only thing you'll remember from this lunch.

It is important to **recognize** who works in the company. Whether it is name tags, uniform shirts or **uniforms**. Sure you already experienced that when shopped in the store you addressed your question to **somebody** next to you and in the end it was another customer looking for **assistance** as well. In some institutions, they normally use formal uniforms, so it is clearly **visible** at the entrance who **works** there.

The **classic** restaurant usually has a **permanent** menu and menu of the day. Specialized restaurants have their own menu and offer **specialties**. If you have a pancake shop and offering a **fresh** bean soup daily, you may **attract** the attention, . The main thing is to have a menu that is **interesting** and is all **prepared** from fresh ingredients.

Staff can be **trained** and educated. Daily at 15 minute meetings, always talk about **different** topic for business. You can learn the **techniques** of preparing, serving the food and **treating** the guests. **Every** member of the team from cook to assistant waiter **must** have a **knowledge** about the menu and **all** ingredients. This is very **important** not only from a professional point of view but also for the **safety** of guests with different eating habits.

Today the restaurants are visited by **many** clients with **allergies**, in tolerances and they have **special** requirements. The basic types of food preparation specifications are:

- **Gluten free die**t – not to use anything that contains gluten
- **Lactose-free diet** – not to use anything that contains lactose (milk sugar)
- **Vegetarian diet** - ingredients of vegetable origin are used - eggs, cheese can be used after agreement with the client
- **Vegan diet** - only pure vegetable products and raw products are used
- **Pescatarian** - clients who consume vegetarian food and fish
- **Excluding dairy products** – not to use any milk, butter, cream, yoghurt in any form
- **Saltsylates** - natural chemicals present in food in the form of additives - nuts, fruits, vegetables, tea, coffee, spices and honey, these foods must be kept out
- **Amino diet** - histamine, a substance found in fermented foods, citrus, avocado, beer, wine, smoked fish, vinegar - everything that the client lists
- **Molluscs, fish** - this includes seafood, fish and all products of them
- **Nuts and peanuts**
- **Legumes and soya**
- **Eggs and products of it**
- **Sulphites** - are found mainly in wine and canned foods

It also **includes** religious eating habits, diabetics, postoperative people, clients with high blood pressure who limit salt and others

There are **many** other types of allergies and intolerances. In the US they also have a special institute that issues **certificates** to all catering staff. Clients therefore **know** that eating in a restaurant is **safe** even though they have **different** diet restrictions.

These **certificates** also give **credit** to restaurants and facilities.

All **special** requests and allergies must be **verified** with a customer before each order. Every restaurant employee **needs** to know these basic things and **communicate** it with a customers. It is necessary to study and know **all** this information. From cooks, waiters to managers and owners.

Do you know what makes a **difference** from the average waiter to best – HERO? Hero **carries** a notepad and **writes** the orders. It is not important to **remember** everything, it is important to know where to **find** what we do not remember. In **hospitality**, this is a double true.

It's really comical but sad as the waiter approaches the table, puts the non-alcoholic beer in front of the daughter and the son doesn't get the plate because someone "forgot". It happens and very often. This is one of the requirements for perfect service and customer satisfaction. Yes, this experience will be remembered by the family for a long time, but will NOT return. Now you know why.

Necessary equipment of the HERO waiter:

- **clean and presenting appearance**
- **pleasant smell**
- **SMILE** as part of the uniform, always present
- **Notebook** - if it is not electronic with direct connection to the kitchen, paper is sufficient - representative! not a kind of trouble to scratch something and not to read
- **writing pen** (preferably with a company logo) and at least 3 - yes three, because someone always needs to "borrow" it and usually does not return - but if we have a business, at least advertising is guaranteed
- **bottle and wine opener**
- **matches** - even in non-smoking operation, because they are always needed and again best with the company logo
- **crumber** if you have a tablecloths - this impresses everyone, it's a part of the impression on the customer and the transformation of feeling into money - about this later on
- **willingness to listen**

Many misunderstandings in the restaurants and bars cause from the fact that the staff does not **listen** to the client. If we **find out** at the **first** moment that a customer has **specific** requirements, we need to pay **attention**. Sometimes very **little** is enough for a client to leave excited and **happy**, sometimes very little to **makes** him leave angry and not come back anymore

Listen carefully to what the client asks you to do. If the requests are unusual, do not answer immediately that it is not possible but ask the supervisor or the chef in the kitchen if it can be done. In one place they served all dishes on wooden plates, only pizza was not. The customer especially requested porcelain. However, the waiter did not want to ask the chef and the customer left.

It is only a problem of **communication** that can be **trained**. Tell the customer that you will **find** out. In full operation, it is very **important** to learn to **recognize** priorities. Customers who have finished are **fine** to wait a few minutes for the bill, as those ones who ordered half an hour ago and have not **received** anything yet. If the kitchen really does not **catch up**, it is good to offer customers something **"Extra"**. Even if they did not order the appetizer, it is always a good idea to have **prepared** a plates- small sandwiches, the guests will be entertained and the kitchen will **gain** time which needed.

This way you will not lose the **trust** of your clients and they will certainly wait next time and maybe order and **pay** for the starter themselfs. Do not panic. This usually **happens** also in the best restaurants . Therefore, it is always necessary to have plan B. Even an **extra** pot of soup served if **necessary** will help. If you have sorbet at your menu and the main meal is out of sight, serve it as an intermezzo - that is a small palet-cleaning break. The guests **will** thank you, **wait** and don't even notice that the preparation of the main meal took 20 minutes more than usual.

When serving the food and drinks, it is important to always present and name the dishes. The lady ordered a pepper chicken, so we give it to her with the words "Madam, your pepper chicken". This makes the professional HERO different from the others. I know the case when the guest ordered a plate, the waiter brought it and the food was presented as follows: the guest asks "and what is it? "And the waiter answers "what you ordered" ... the client got his food on the plate presented in a way he had never seen before and the waiter didn't even know what he was serving. This also happens. But not to HERO! He will learn and lead by example!

If you have a **reservation** system in the restaurant and you can **regulate** at least weekends and lunches, **congratulations**. However, if you have an **open** system the first comes, the first served ... please **keep** it. It often happens that **clients** who have been seated after you will be served first or preferably. In the eyes of the **customer**, it is neither nice nor **professional**.

Ensure that you have a **proper** record of arrivals and orders. If you are not able attend the guest in the **standard** waiting time frame, **explain it**. If you are **preparing** the meals according to **special** orders or potatoes needs a bit longer cooking time ... there will be no problem if you **explain** it to the client. It also **happens** that client ordered something you are just running out of in the kitchen. Do not be affraid and **talk** to the guest. Honesty and truth is the **best** way in any business.

You can **offer** an alternative or even a **specialty** of the restaurant at the price of the meal **originally** ordered. The client will certainly return to you and tell this to **everyone** else – you get **free** advertising and a **loyal** client for **sure**.

Introduce a **quality** valuation system for your customers – survey. Leave the **cards** at the entrance door, at the desk, at the checkout **where** your customers can see them and **write** the comments. **Talk** to the guests to **see** what they liked and what you could **improve**.

Today is possible also to have an **electronic** form – questionaire. There are many evaluation **portals** where you can set up your survey also for free.

A few years ago I advised this to one of the facilities where they organized a children's summer camp. They have not been able to fill the camp for last 5 years. So after the first two 7-days turns we sent out e-mails with questionnaires to all parents. And it was a surprise what the answer came back. We learned that one of the instructors was not nice at all, the chocolate buns were low in sugar and were bitter, and half of the children did not wash their hands before lunch.

As you can see in the example, **communication** is the base.

3. LEARN, LEARN AND LEARN…

You will face clients for the **first** time. It's a great **feeling**. You've come all the way here and it's up to you how quickly you get **involved** in the work process. **Everything** needs to be followed, repeat, ask. Only then you will **learn** what you **need.** There is a different system in every job and **everything** is new at the beginning.

There will be **a lots** of informations. Write down everything you can. Best **practice**, however. When you do that **daily**, you become an **expert**. Always **study** something. If there is a option and employer **provides** training and courses, sign up. It **can be** a language course, marketing strategy or communication. Education **must** be kept in mind at all the times. There is **always** something to learn, to **improve**.

Use the Internet, search, study. There is **a lots** of informations around , the **right** ones will always **reach** you.

And now something about **providing** the service. Whether it's a bar or a restaurant, the **rules** are the same. This is not new to those skilled in the business, but it is **very** important for those who just started. It is actually the **base** of success. **Proper** timing and procedures are **important** for smooth **operation** and especially client **satisfaction**.

Remember what was **offered** to you **first** in your favorite restaurant. After sitting - where we will of course help the ladies, children and the elderly we **offer** them our menu - food and beverage menu, if we have it prepared separately. Be **aware** that any menu is also an **advertisement** of your business or establishment . Therefore, it should **always** be clean, without torn and written on pages.

It **should** contain as much **informations** as possible about the food and drinks served - composition, origin, allergens. The **more** information is on the menu, the **fewer** questions the clients will have. It is **always** good to have the name of the owner, manager or chef.

We are always approaching the **first** older ladies. If we have **children** at the table, we give them **primary** attention. When serving the **family**, we always preffer to **bring** drinks and meals to the **smallest** members. **Children** up to the age of 11-12 years serve **first** and then we continue to the rest of the family in **order** - older ladies, other women, older gentlemen, other gentlemen.

If we have a **host** at the table, the father of the family, the celebrant , he tastes the wine **first**, but the food is served to him **last**. First we **always** offer the drinks. If the client orders **sparkling** wine, this is served **first**. You can also **offer** an aperitif or a cocktail. The wine is served first white and then red. The wine is **offered** for tasting **immediately** after opening the bottle to the **host** or the **oldest** gentleman.

Remember that champagne comes from the Champagne region of France and it is the **only** wine that has naturally formulated bubbles in a bottle and the name Champagne can only be **used** for wines from this region. Other wines are **sparkling** and carbonated (CO_2) during the production process and then bottled. These are **offered** under the name **sparkling**. The **price** of these drinks will also depend on this.

White wine is **recommended** to serve with white meat, desserts. Red wine is served with a dark meat and venison. The **names** of the wines are formed from the **grape variety** from which they are made. White: tramin, risling, pinot grigio, chardonay. The reds can be: pinot noir, barolo, malbec. Then they are mixtures of wines and special "blends" where everyone can choose according to their own taste.

You can serve **local wine** in traditional carafe or flavored Spanish sangria in a pitcher. You can also offer homemade lemonade with lemon, elder flower or mint flavour. **Bottled drinks** must always be presented to the client with the label up and opened in **front** of the guests at the table. This applies not only to wine, soft drinks but also to mineral waters.

You'll make **sure** everyone gets their ordered drink and you'll go to take a food order. The **same** rule applies as for the drinks. First take the order from **children, older ladie**s, etc. It is always necessary to maintain eye contact and write the order so that it can be readable. Sure you had the honor to meet the waiters "dudes" who did not write anything and then it looked like. There were mushrooms in the omelette - your son hates this and the daughter on the diet got potatoes even she ordered rice.

If the guest have a **questions**, try to answer **truthfully**. If you are unsure, apologize and ask your supervisor or chef. This rule applies **double** to clients with allergies or special requirements. If everything is written, move the order into the kitchen.

Always remember to serve the clients in the **order** they were seated. This will avoid misunderstandings. If the preparation **takes** longer, tell the guest. Be **honest**. If you have time, take your part in the easy conversation. **Ask** the guest how was his day, whether he was in the restaurant for the first time or who recommended it to him.

When serving bread and butter or spreads or other snacks in the restaurant at the beginning, bring this **as soon** as you take the order along with the drinks. Present everything nicely and name it. Mention that it is **included** in the price, guests will be pleased.

If the offered bread, butter, spreads and snacks are not included, **inform** the guests. This way, the client has a choice and you avoid misunderstandings.

Serve food as soon as it is ready, do not wait. Prepare the table for the next course with **time reserve**. The client will forgive you five minutes of extra waiting for the food preparation, but never cold food.

The basis is to listen **carefully** and **fulfill** the wishes of customers in the shortest possible time. With a **smile** you will always achieve **more** than a long face expression even if the order is complicated in any way. Hold the sarcastic notes and jokes. It is **worth** it. Face expression has more value than you think.

The following is a part that is not very popular but is most needed. **Guest complaints** - don't be stressed. You are here to learn how to **handle unexpected situations** and with calm.

Do not interrupt your guest when is already complaining. **Listen** to everything and wait until the guest stop or ask you something. If you're the manager, **offer solution**. If you have a supervisor **inform** the guest that you need to speak to him and contact your supervisor immediately.

Manager, no matter what he is doing, he has an **obligation** to come to the guest as quickly as possible. Listen to him, agree completely and show empathy, understanding. He need to **apologize**, politely with patience.

Of course, a **solution** must be offered. All problems have a solution. In practice I have verified that you just need to listen to the client and then ask what he suggests. 99% of complainers **don't even know** what they really want. With the question what is **expecting**, you will win it.

With experience in the future you will be able to read the client from the beginning. Sometimes it is enough to offer **a refund**, something extra or simply credit it to the business budget. Vouchers for a discount for **next visit** have also proven success - you have your money, the client will come back and you can be sure that the next time the complaint is not going to happen.

Always remember to **thank** the client for the feedback. If a guest is **right** - and sometimes he really is - it's actually good that he expressed himself. At least you can work on **improvement**. Constructive criticism must always be accepted. It is one of the **ways to success**. And it is good if the client speaks **directly** to you and you will not find out about it in the newspaper or on the Internet.

It is always necessary to **return** to the client and it does not matter whether you or your supervisor handled the complaint. Ask again if he is **satisfied** with the outcome of the complaint. When you learn this and take personal **responsibility** , this shows your **professionalism**.

Always **inform** the client about everything that is happening. Whether you need to talk to a manager or prepare something special, always let him know. **Ask** for a moment of patience - you can also say that you need approximately 15 minutes, but **always keep** this time frame.

Abroad, it is common for large coroporations as well as small businesses to have their **black list.** There are **notes** about any dissatisfied or troubled clients. The nightclubs also have restricted entry notes.Some companies simply **refuse you services.**

If you can **register** your clients it is easier. If not, you need to rely on the good memory of the workers. In my practice it happened that we had a photos of offending clients **posted** on the notice board. And then it is clear that John was surprised that everyone knew him when he almost demolished the restaurant a few months ago.

This is a very sensitive topic, but you have to protect yourself and your employees. Abroad, in some countries and resorts, there are internal online lists where "troubled" clients can be found. Whenever you encounter such a situation, make a more detailed record of the situation. Sometimes circumstances require the police assistance.

4. CUSTOMER NEEDS

Some clients come and don't even know what they **expect**. It's up to you to get them where you **want** them to be. The client arrives undecided and waits for your **offer**. You as a professional must first **know your product** in detail and then learn the sales techniques where the **result** is 100 percent **guaranteed**. The client needs to be convinced that your service or product is what he needs and has never known it .

If we got the client **attention** from the first time, he will **come back** to us. And he will bring with him a family, friends. When he organizes a celebration and your establishment offers this, he will certainly contact you. Only - he must know about it first. Therefore, it is always good to **mention** what celebrations you can organize just between speech each time you submit an check. Not only do we give **information** but we also do advertising - for free. It is good to have this information in printed form on tables or on promotional items that the customer can take away - matches, pens and also on the website. Everything we have **in sight** we might need one day.

My friend used to go to a restaurant for lunch. In winter, when there were fewer customers, the owner got the idea to bake and offer homemade cakes. At first for the weekend, and later also during the week, after some time the offer expanded to include fresh desserts. My friend already regularly orders all kinds of cakes for celebrations, holidays, weddings. The message spread very quickly and today the owner has a steady secondary income throughout the year and the business has helped to overcome the difficult period.

There are infinitely many tips and **ideas**. Also rent unused congress hall for social events on weekends, providing production capacity of the kitchen for various **occasions** - ready meals, desserts, cold dishes, canapés.

Today, it should be a **certain matter** that every facility in hospitality has more functions and offers **more** services. Abroad, it is common for a small hotel owner to invest in the purchase of 8 seats vehicles and to offer clients trips around the area by his own . Alternatively, he works with someone who offers such **services** and agrees on a sales commission. In the seaside areas, they even offer boat trips, whether sightseeing or fishing.

In one hotel, cooks also helped prepare and distribute ready to eat meals. Immediately in the morning they always prepare 200 portions of vacuum-packed food which will be picked up by bus drivers, taxi drivers and shop assistants from nearby shops around 11am. Even before they open the restaurant for public lunch, they have their daily income already secured.

And you can **offer** all this to clients on your place. Even through your website. The web is actually your advertising. List there what you offer. **Organization** of meetings, parties, weddings, transport of the guests, distribution of food and drinks, daily offer. The more **interesting** and colorful your web is, the better.

When you choose where to go on **vacations** to relax, you will always be interested more in hotels and facilities **with pictures**, description. In this spirit, also present yourself, your business. Put yourself in the customer's needs to **better define** the services you can offer.

Keep an eye on social networks - market sites, **especially** those around you, and **offer** your services in an interesting way. Free advertising exists on every social network. Yes there is also paid one, but you can start **for free**. You reach out to **everyone** you know and then they send an ad to their friends. That's how it works in the world.

Of course there are exceptions. Why would I extend a neighbor's ad to his car repair. He has enough money, so why is he **advertising** ... these are some of our practices. But if your car breaks down, you go to neighbor John. Because you know him and know that he does **quality** job and fast.

This is precisely because you **understand** the needs of the customer and you do not need to advertise your operation. Trust in a well done job is the **best advertising**.

The hair studio on the edge of town still has full appointments. There's a great young lady working there. You can talk to her about anything, she offers you a hair mask you didn't even know you needed. Did you burn your hair with an inappropriate color on Friday night? Never mind, she runs to you on Saturday and you don't have to worry all weekensd how you go to see your colleagues on Monday. And believe it, you don't even want to go have your hair done somewhere else. You have the best service there.

Of course, from the above, if you understand the psychology of non forced **natural sales**, you will surely succeed. It's also about doing something **"extra"** and the client will stay with you. Where he is taken care of and feels comfortable, he will certainly **return again**.

The sooner you realize the customer's needs, the sooner you build regular clients.

5. KNOW YOUR CLIENT

Services are always about **providing** the best **feeling** to the client. Who asks a lot will learn a lot. In the beginning, always **let the client** talk. You will **find out** what he actually expects and demands, you can better meet his expectations and it will be a **win - win** "relationship". So that the client will gladly return to you and recommend you further. Satisfaction is on **both** sides.

It is necessary to **listen** to the client's **needs** in every business, but **double** in hospitality. Our business, **our profits** and our reputation grow with client satisfaction. These factors are the most **important**. In the hospitality sector, most clients are in relaxation pose. However, if it is not a broken car that needs to be repaired very **quickly**, or a hungry driver who has fallen asleep on the road. Then you better be **careful**.

However, this is also our topic. We **can estimate** the client at the first moment. But do not **be fooled** by appearances. Even a man in a overall who has just entered your car dealer shop can have 40,000 euros in cash with him to buy a new car. / a real example from a well-known brand store /

Clients **come** mainly to satisfied their needs with our **service**. They're looking for something we can certainly **offer** to them if they've come to our door. It is up us to **find a solution** for client and keep him. We need to be prepared for the conversation from which the **business** will come. An interview at the end of which we will **close the deal**.

These things can be learned. Conducting **business** conversations, offering solutions, **closing** conversations. In service needs to be acted quickly. Usually you have only one try. Therefore, it is necessary to **prepare** well in advance and **increase** the percentage of success.

The more you **know** about the client, the better you will work. Ask and **listen**. Offer a solution and **leave** the decision to the client. **Never** force him into anything. When people feel we **care** about them and offer a **solution** to their problem, they make their own decisions, and mostly for **your** benefit.

The offered **solution** is to give the client a free **choice**, and that means for you that whatever the client chooses, you will both **benefit** from it.

First of all, **clarify** with the client his idea. **Find out** in advance what the competition offers. This way you will know exactly what you can offer differently or in **addition** and be sure that the client will choose **your** service, product.

Two restaurants opposite each other offer organizing celebrations. Both are known for quality food and service. The prices are almost the same but ... one offers something extra. It can be decoration of the hall, music, animation program, just about anything. By the time the second company wakes up, the first one is busy for the next month.

It is important to **alternate** the offer, look for new solutions and ideas. Sometimes you just need to **switch** suppliers and you can go down with the price of a product or service. Conversely, you can offer **better** quality after switching supplier. This is the case, for example, with coffee and drinks. You will **change** your brand and your business will be more **occupied** and therefore you make more revenue and **profit**.

A large wedding agency organized spectacular celebrations. Every Saturday they were busy for months ahead. However, they found out that they only need 2 full days for preparation. They started offering snacks in large companies and institutions in the city from Monday to Thursday, offering cold meals and hot drinks every day at a specified time, and still having a free Sunday. They got to know their clients and their habits and made the satisfaction of everyone involved.

In the nail studio worked two ladies who took turns. They were friends and the same age. However, one listened carefully to her clients, writing down their names, and asked in conversations what colors the customer liked best, what style of clothing she preferred to work. After half a year she started to have many regular clients and took the new ones based only on recommendations . The other lady gave up, took a job at the hotel where the reception organizing her clients. She has a fixed fixed salary and so it suits her.

Personal **interest** in the client has been here since ever. The better relationship you build, the stronger the **roots** of your business. In hospitality, it is important to build a strong **database** of clients.

In one sports shop 20 years ago the saleswoman wrote down loyal clients, who searched for news and wanted to be always informed about new goods that came into the store. Over time, this database has changed to electronic and today before the summer season, the bicycles are sold before they arrive at the store, in winter they sell ski equipment and in fact something is found every month.
Clients get used to and trust that they always get the best.

6. HOW TO EXCHANGE A FEELINGS FOR MORE MONEY

The hospitality sells a **feeling** as an final product. How guests felt with us will be long in their **memory**. The better we engage and satisfy, the **better** the feeling will be. And for a good feeling, people are **willing to pay**. And much more than you thought so far.

For example, such a taxi. You need a transfer. Taxi driver greets you nice, opens the door. How do you feel? Okay, right? The taxi driver stretches his legs to help you load and unload your suitcase. You have a fantastic feeling and leave him more than he asked for.

Hospitality **open** up the client's heart and wallet. If the client gets more than **expected**, you will get more than you expected. And this **applies** to all services. Hairdressers, restaurants, hotels, taxis.

Remember your last **vacation**. How was it? What **impressions** did it leave in you? Are you **looking forward** to the next year and have you booked the **same** hotel? And why? The answer is simple - you **felt comfortable**. Therefore, you will gladly return and surely recommend this place to your friends.

In hotels and restaurants, if a guest feels **cared for**, he will be **generous** to you. You do not have to receive only cash, it can be various gift items, vouchers or event tickets. The client will come **back** to you again and will **reward** you the way you did not expect .

For hospitality workers in all positions, it is important and generally applicable:
- **Personal hygiene**
- **Clean and presenting clothes**
- **Fresh breath**
- **Pleasant smell**
- **Smile on the face**

Are you asking how all this is related to **business**?... Very related! When a client enters your facility and finds a **presentable**, nice staff with whom they will feel **comfortable**, will certainly return. And it doesn't matter in which area you work or do business. If you work there and you are the first person the client meets, it's even more important. According to Forbes / famous american business magazine/ **first impression** lasts 7 seconds and matters 93% of what we see and hear. The remaining 7% is what we say. Of course we are waiting for **success**, so we need to be **prepared**.

The client often forgets what we told him or what he saw. But the way he felt with us will **remain most engraved** in his memory. Feelings are the most important and remain the longest. Most of our lives developped from feelings. We are begin to realize this in the 21st century. We care more about our body, what we eat, what we drink. We go to massages, beauty centers, gyms and restaurants.

More emphasis is placed on a healthy **lifestyle** and.... Feeling of satisfaction, happiness, love. We learn to relax more, relieve the mind from stress and **"enjoy"**. FEELING. We are willing to pay for this. And not a little. We look for the **best** facilities to get the best service.

What is the best service?

Sometimes is enough a friendly **smile**, exchange of a few words. This is the key to the client's heart and **wallet**. It means that if the client felt **comfortable** with us, next time he would come with the whole family, he would recommend us further and we have new clients that we have to take care of to return to us and **bring** us clients even more.

It is a simple time-tested system. For example: there are two restaurants side by side in the city. One is always full and the other is empty. They have a similar offer but are different. Sometimes the price for the services also makes a difference. If Mary brings you a beer with a smile and even throws a funny comment, you're sure to pay a few cents more and go back there

John has a better and cheaper beer but Mary gives it to you with something extra and it's basically free - a human approach. In hospitality human touch is most important. Each restaurant or hotel is similarly equipped. They have tables, chairs, beds, curtains. They can also be expensive from cheaper material, but it always depends on how the staff taking care of us. Even a towel in the fitness center can just be given you, or you can get it with a simple smile and words "here is your towel please". The whole future and the client's decision-making are then followed up from this approach. Your success depend of that.

In the introduction it was mentioned a "crumbs scraper" /crumber/ which will do his part. It is something I have met only abroad so far. After the main meal the waiter comes to clean the table and cleans the crumbs from the table cloth. These professionals received **30% more money** from guests than those who did not.

This is a way how to convert the feeling for more money. Your money. Sell the FEELING. It pays off for you !!!

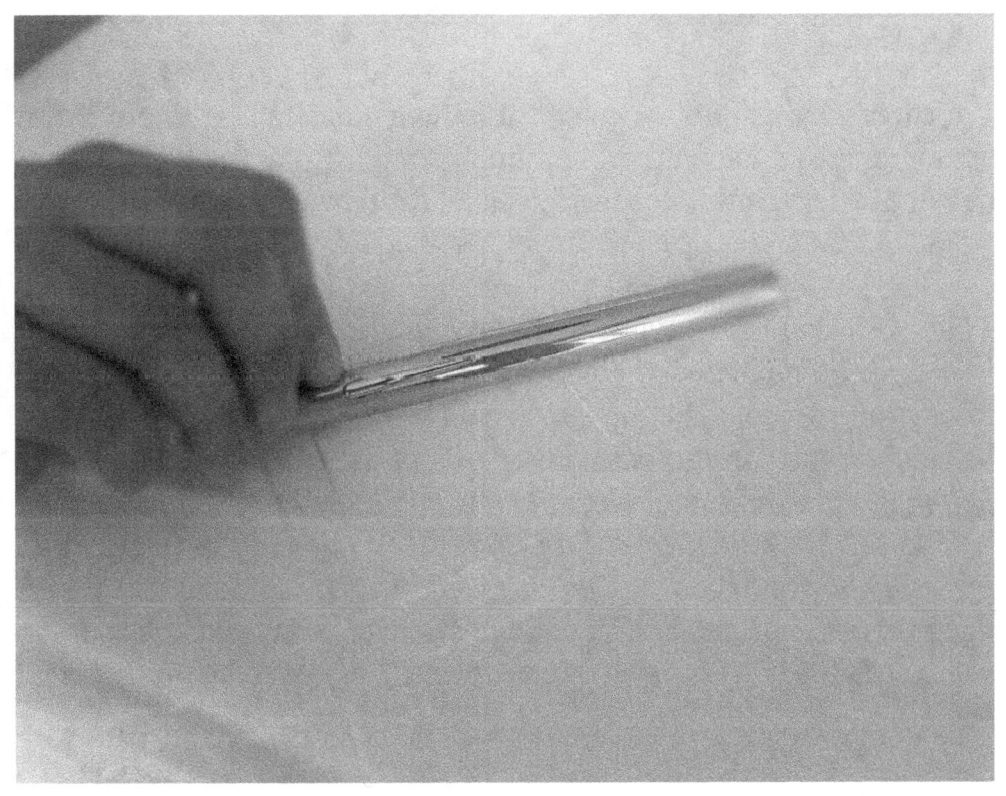

7. SUCCESS WILL COME – JUST KEEP GOING

With a **positive** attitude, smile on your face and great service, your work and business will surely cultivate and succeed. **Professionals** repeat their **skills** every day and learn new ones. They listen carefully, get advices, do not make unreasonable decisions.

The task of a professional is to stay, become better and **give** his experience to young ones. The more with a heart, the better. Help and motivation should be given as granted. Then the professional becomes a leader. One with **natural authority** and respect. Everything comes gradually, naturally.

We **copy** what is good - we can **improve** what can be improved. A person does not become professional from one day to other. Once is developped, is getting respect. Respect for himself and others.

I have a friend who studied engineering. He worked as a developer in a large manufacturing company. He had different ideas about the job as the company management. So after some time he decided to help his brother in the bakery. He was at the start of the company, helping with everything, learning. He suddenly just thought to start baking bread in the shape of a flower. Everyone laughed at him and teased him. The bread began to be sold in bulk. Although it was a few cents more expensive. He added sweet pastries and cakes of the same shape. He did not give up, diversed himself from others and persist.

From ZERO to HERO   LINDA ZAMBRANO DACHOVA

It doesn't matter where you started and what you did. You can **always** become a professional in the area that **you enjoy** even if it looks crazy. You need **to go** for your goal and not give up. Success **comes**.

Someone think of **success** as being famous and showing up. Someone needs to have a work results and be proud of them. It's **individual**. But always choose the option that **fills you** with happiness, satisfaction and good feeling.

Only then you will **become** a professional. Only this strong **motivation** will drive you forward and **help you** overcome barriers. Important is to **keep going**.

Both large and small companies have **success** and tripping. Learn, stand up and **move on**. Once you have your destination, you will surely arrive there. No matter how long it takes, the goal is yours. And it's **up to you**. Over time, you may **change** your goal. It is also up to you.

My friend Leni always wanted to be the director of a big company. She studied economics and foreign trade. She worked and worked on her career. After years she worked her way up to deputy director. She traveled, educated, led her team of experts. The day came when she met Martin and married. When Mike was born, she worked from home. After a year she returned to the company. She was offered a job she had dreamed of for so long - a director's job. Lenka, however, decided something else. She remained in her original position. Her goals changed and she knew it. With her original position she can plan her work better and has more time for her family. She still works in the same company.

Being the HERO is simple. Honest and professional.

8. CRUISE SHIPS – BEST HOSPITALITY

It is actually a **special** chapter that needs to be described in more details. It's not **new** and it's become popular. Cruise business is one of the **most organized** form of hospitality. Multi billions business. Service is more up and more **different** from anything you ever experienced.

Over the years, I have learned that **anyone** who wants to do this job can do it. It's difficult- YES, but the **result** is worth it. Have you always wanted to travel and have a regular income? It is possible. You just have to **want to**. The industry has **changed** in recent years. And for the better. There are more professionals than in any other industry in the world. It's actually a floating city where is **everything**. From accommodation, through the restaurants, bars, shops, hospital, laundry, power plant, water purifier and even a tailor.

Companies **gives a job** to people up to 67 years old - that was the oldest crew member I ever met. So everybody really have a chance. There is a **minimum** requierement - good health certified by a worldwide medical certificate, language skills at the communicative level - English, German or Spanish and especially **willingness** to do.

Many of today's top managers **started** in the kitchen by washing dishes or cleaning public areas. Today, after a few years, they have **developed**. The motivation is therefore strong. Just don't give up. Language can also be learned. And very fast. There are various online applications where you will catch it so that in a fun way you will **learn** everything necessary - busuu, duolingo.

So stop to have an excuses about everything because **the real** problem is only you. . It's up to you what you decide. **Ask** yourself what you really enjoy. This makes it easier to **find** the way to go. My eBook **How to Get a Dream Job**, which is free to download, will also inspire you. www.worldoflinda.sk

To be a **HERO** in this environment you need to start with **basic**.Service onboard is just – **different**. Huge competition of the companies require to hire the **BEST** possible. All mentioned from the first page of this eBook you can use.

Hotel at the cruise ship:

You need to be **physically** fit to work in a hotel. Bed sheets are changing every day and balconies should be also cleaned **daily**. The client will forgive you dust but never dirt. Hair, papers and bottles under the bed, forgotten personal belongings, that's what you **need** to **watch out** for.

But ... on the first day you usually **replace** the worker who was there before you. So you are immediately **expected** to take on your tasks. There is no time to learn and explain. If you come as a public cleaner, they'll give you a vacuum cleaner in your hand and **show** you what you need to clean. The same thing happens when you come as a maid to clean the rooms.

Once you've manage the basic habits and **find the system**, other will go easy. The base is done, you can develop another site - your progress or improving the communication. When you get on, you always get a **job description** and an explanation of what to do.

You get into it and learn as you go. One thing is for sure - use **logic** and common sense. That everything is sometimes in a foreign environment and foreign language does not matter. Start cleaning as normal. It starts from **above to below**. Then vacuum and wipe off the dust on the **end.** If you do the opposite, you will have dust again after vacuuming all around.

Your supervisor will **require** a lot. Through a clean and neat bed, vacuumed carpets, wiped dust and door frames to a clean balcony. You should also be **careful** about refrigerators and their interior. This should also **always** be checked. It is important to catch everything **before** the arrival of guests.

If you are the one on **supervisor** role, you know what to check. Everything needs to be **spotless**. Supervisor can inspect also with a rug in his hand. This is not a shame. Is a **lead** by example.

You **meet** your guests on the first day. HERO **makes sure** he does. Usually only briefly. You introduce yourself and give them a contact where they can **always** reach you. It is important to ask first whether they have any **special** requirements or wishes. **Write** everything down !!! Room number, names and requirements. This way you can **check** daily that everything is **in order** and you will not forget anything.

Wishes can be **different** - always full buckets with ice, always clean towels, extra shampoo, soap. But you might also **find** the following:
- if guests like to sleep in the morning - you will **know** that you will clean their room later
- plans for the next day - you can plan **your** cleaning better
- sometimes **tell you** that you only need to change your bed linen after 3 days and not every other
- likes to order breakfast in the room - you must **always** come to take used dishes on time

There is also evening service on the ship, when you can **find out** the following:
- when the guests go to dinner - you can finish faster when most tell you their program - but you **have to talk** to the guests
- sometimes they don't want to be disturbed in the evening - so you have less cabins :)

This knowledge will make your working life much easier. You can **plan** things better and finish sooner. **Communication** is the most important thing. Try to keep in touch with the client at least once a day, or you can make a courtesy phone call. You ask the client what you can do. **Never** ask if everything is all right, you only get a yes or no answer. It is necessary to communicate so that the client responds with a **longer sentence**. From this you can decide if you can **offer** something more.

Clients usually remembers a **first impression**. After opening the hotel room door, it should look clean, **organized** and spotless. The sticky rounds from the cups on the table or in the bathroom look very unprofessional. In this work, **learn** that what looks clean may not be clean. Everything needs to **be checked**. And twice minimum.

There are various stories and myths about the cruise ships. But it is a very **professional** job like no other. It is related with **travel**, precision, punctuality. In the restaurant and the hotel you do not enjoy much sleep, so if less than 8 hours a day is not enough, you can **train** yourself or better look for something else - casino, bar, shops. There you usually work with small breaks for 12 hours at a time and then you have the rest of the time free. But again it will be mainly about night work.

Work skills can be **learned**, work habits can be trained. You will learn everything you need and especially very **quickly**. Cruise ship - this is **24-hour operation**. Even when you sleep, someone works. Day and night. A floating **city** that is always in motion.

Work is **at least** 10 hours a day, 7 days a week from 4 to 9 months. Weekends - do not exist, in the true sense of the word, but you have time to relax. This counts for **hours**. It's up to you how you organize it. You have the **opportunity** to get to know the world - if you are docked in the port and you have time off - or refresh and relax when you sail on the sea and have time off.

So it's primarily a job that is **worth it**. However, it depends on your position how much you will **save** in your account each month. **Basically** you get at least $ 600 per month. You can stay all the time in a given starting position, or get **promoted** and earn more. All depends of your knowledge, experiences and **willingness**.

Professionals have higher salaries, depending on education, experiences and the negotiation skills at the interview.
Salaries are as follows (all approximate) in US dollars: / source - Google /
- assistant waiter 1400
- waiters 2200
- the fourth cook 800
- second cook 1600
- bartenders 1800
- bar waiters 1500
- electricians 1200
- waterworks 1400

- vendors in shop 1200
- casino dealers 1200
- Youth Adviser 1400
- Travel Agent 1500
- hotel staff 1000
- steward 2000
- Butler 1800
- massage therapist 1400
- Manicurist 1400
- hairdresser 1400

And then there are managerial positions:

- Head of division 4000
- leading managers 5000 - 8000
 and higher management is paid even better….

In addition to the above is possible to receive the **tips** where the amount can be up to **twice** what you officially receive. So, as a new assistant waiter, you **can add** another thousand to your paycheck per month.

This may **vary** from the company and your experience. In any case, it is **worth** trying. It's a lot of effort and self discipline, but it's beautiful. Travel around the world and get **paid for** it. If you have a family, this step will be even harder for you.

But believe that **70%** of the crew have families at home and there are companies that giving a job to **couples**. If you have children, and place where you can leave them and you think you can handle those **6 months** without them, you need to go after **your dream**. There are also river cruises companies that offers a seasonal work for 2 to 3 months.

Choosing the right job means identifying what you enjoy and able to manage. If you are unsure about your **knowledge**, you need to **apply** for general work. There are positions of public area cleaners, room cleaners, assistant chefs. Here you can **improve** your language and by the time you can apply for a **better** paid job.

In a few months you will **achieve** everything you have dreamed of. You will return **home** with a fantastic **feeling** and money in your pocket. Attention - this work is highly addictive. It's actually a **lifestyle**. Hard work, **discipline** on the one hand - **travel** and money on the other. Even if you invest something at the beginning, it will **return** multiple times.

The crew is **multicultural**. Roommates and colleagues will be from all over the world. What is **normal** for one may not be for another. People grew up in **other** cultures, religions, with other habits. Respect and tolerance are the most **important**. The **general** rules of good conduct apply.

In this environment there are also many **friendships** that can last for years. Here are mostly people you spend a **lot of time** with, and sometimes you don't know **anything** about them. Even after six months when you go home. And there are the others that after 20 years you still **visit** them and keep **in touch** over the half world.

You will **learn** new things from **colleagues** you work with. One is an English teacher and will forever teach and correct you, the other is a **professional** bartender and teaches you the secret of mixing drinks so that even after 10 years his recipe will still **make you** a money. Here is all about team work. Showing your **own** responsibility and honesty is **the best**.

You will follow this path and **success** is guaranteed. The management will notice you, guests will five you a good comments and you have your **way up**. Be yourself and do not pretend or play with anything. Sincerity is **appreciated**.
Help others and **ask** for help yourself. Learn, **share** your ideas and experiences.

It's important to **try** everything. And one thing, when you have the chance to **teach** others something, do it. Next time you don't have to do it and you can do what you need. There is also competition and fights in the international environment. Control the peace, everything which is too much hurts . If you think you need a help, **raise** your hand and you will be **helped**.

If you set an **example**, positivity and good humor, you will achieve your goal. **Learn** from colleagues, supervisors. Experience is gained through years and practice. **Listen t**o the opinions of others, do not interrupt the speech. Do not argue and tell back. Listening is
the base. Speaking Championship.

You will gradually **shape** your personality and character as you adapt and blend in with the crowd **in harmony**. In a game where **victory** is completed job and **satisfaction** of everyone involved. You will grow and your values will gain the importance. You become more **open**. New **knowledge**, experience. Things that were important will suddenly seem irrelevant and you will create new **priorities**. Don't worry, you can do it!

The most difficult will be to **manage** separation from family, friends. Get used to it. You have to. And the **sooner** the better. For you. Accommodation is usually provided by two. **Prepare** that roommate will be from a completely **different** end of the world than you, will have different habits, skin color. The shower will go at night when you sleep and the cologne ... there is always the **possibility** to ask for a change.

Always treat the people nicely. Don't raise your voice, don't shout. Listen to the other end and **learn** patience. This will help you always and everywhere. If you get in touch with your clients over time, you'll **be ahead** of the game. Remember, talking is **good**, but keep silent **better**!

Communication with the outside world will not be as **easy** as you used to. You will only use your mobile phone in your free time and **there is** a business calls ethiquette. Basic phrases "how are you" and "how can I help you?" are common. **Always** introduce yourself by your name. You **never** know who's calling you. It can be a colleague, but also a client.

You chose to work in hospitality, you **need** to give your best. There is a lot of unknown and new things to come. The working environment you are working in is **highly** competitive. There are rules that must be **learned** and followed. You will spend much **more** time at work than you have been used to before.

Start to **learn** positivity. Have a positive attitude to everything. **Smile** and the word NO delete from your dictionary. If you don't understand something, **ask**. There is not a stupid question, just a stupid answer. So **don't worry**. They were all in your place once and learned. The more **questions** you have, the sooner you will **know** everything you need.

Set yourself to an **always** available mode. Every effort is appreciated. If you get a **question** and you can't answer, agree to come up with the answer when you **find out**. There is no shame to ask. Rather, you will be sorry that you do not know something and **admit it** as if you give false information.

Verbal contact must be **adapted** to the new conditions. Polite phrases and **standard** language are very important. Each ship has an official language. It can be English, German, Italian. You will **always** have to communicate in this language officially with a colleague from your country in public. It's a bit **strange** at the beginning, but over time you take it **normally**.

In your **free** time you can communicate in your mother tongue language - if someone understands you. Since some countries are small, you may be the only one there. You will have many **new** friends and will meet a lot of people from **all over** the world. This is an **experience** that will stay with you forever. You will improve in a foreign language, sometimes you will **learn** a new one that you have not even thought about in the past.

Depending on **the size** of the ship and the destination, you can also participate in work that you would not even have thought of before you arrived. **Small** vessels have a **small** team and they **help** each other. In addition to working full-time in the kitchen, you will be assigned to assist in the laundry service, loading of provisions and assisting guests in embarkation and disembarkation with luggage.

This should be clarified before you sign an employment contract. It happened to one of my friend that he did not read it properly, and as the head waiter had to unload the guest's suitcases every week in Europe where this was not the case in the USA. In Europe, on the other hand, you can work 10 hours a day, while in the US it is 14.

It **varies** from company to company, but you always have **everything** in your employment contract. Some companies will pay you a trip to work - they will send you a ticket, somewhere you pay for it yourself. Uniforms you can get, you have to buy them or sometimes bring them from home.

And now to the **benefits** - for food and accommodation you do not pay. Is free. You can **put aside** everything you earn. The job is what it is, but where do you get such a benefits? When you **calculate** it, the amount of working hours may be the same as at home, but on land it is not allowed to work **as much** as at sea.
Night work is also to be expected. Sometimes it is necessary, sometimes workers take turns and you have a night shift only once a while. You need to be **ready** 24 hours, because supervisor can call you to work at **any time** in an **emergency**. Forget free weekend, every day is a Monday. Days of the week don't have a classic name. They called by the ports where the ship is docking. You get used to it quickly.

You don't even know, and time flies very **fast**. You will **learn** everything new first, then you will tune it and look for a system that works best for you. The **discovery** phase takes about 2 months, then the **learning** phase and the last month you will be fully trained.

Before the end of your contract , you **can apply** for another reassignment to the area you have not yet visited. This **way**, in a few years you will go through **everything** that interests you. And what is not ... but it's beautiful. You have the **opportunity** to earn and travel.

Everything described above on the ship you will certainly **need**. In normal operation at a hotel, restaurant, shop or sporting shop, rental, it works the **same** way. The ship is even more interesting and strict. Here, the customers are **recognized** by names – and you too.

This is a **closed** community that opens to new members every 5,7,11,14 days or every month if they are cruising around the world.

Yes, around the world. It's also one of those **advantages** that as a shop assistant or electrician you have the **opportunity** to see the whole world. That's the **difference**.

The demands are **high**, but not impossible. The service area is beautiful. Simple – with **kindness** to honor customers and offer quality service. And always offer something **extra**.

This is the secret of hospitality …….

9. STORIES FOR INSPIRATION

During my career I have met people from all over the world. Everyone was gone from their home country, they came to work to help families, themselves. The goal is always one - **customer satisfaction and your satisfaction**. Feeling good at work, earning the money you deserve.

People has a different **motivation**. I met a couple from the Philippines who came to earn for a new house and start their own business. There was also an Indian who, in 30 years time, had **employed** the whole family in 3 family hotels they own, a girl from Russia who wanted to see the world or a young man from Colombia whose father is a bank manager and he **wanted** to become independent without his help.

Natallia: Belarus

When I was a child, I always dreamed that one day I would see the world, visit different countries and meet a lot of people. When I was 10, I knew exactly what I need to do to make my dreams true. I was studying English day and night in order to speak to foreigners as English is the most popular language nowadays. I entered the Minsk State Linguistic University at the English Faculty to pursue my dream. One day a young lady came and told us that if u wanted to travel the world, u should go to work on a cruise ship. And that was it. I was going through different cruise lines and the most charming one for me was Celebrity. And this is it. I passed the interview. And then just before my birthday I got a contract to be part of the best team on the fleet. In September 2014 I became an employee of Celebrity Cruises. I started as an assistant waitress and I lived that job. So many guests of different nationalities were passing during my contract and I was enjoying talking to them. And then I got the opportunity to move forward in my carrier. That was great. I made my training for the hostess. And that is it. I am proud to be a Restaurant Hostess on Celebrity Summit. And I am happy that Celebrity Cruises made my dreams to come true.

Cesar – Costa Rica:

I was 18 years old studying English and a lousy job ,but still looking for a better one , a escape from my boring life , i can do more i was thinking at the time , one day i opened the news paper and there it was the dream job, seemed too far
but close at the same time ,i applied immediately , i waited 4 months to get an answer , are you still interested?- finally came- i ran to the place and i was accepted on the spot i was given 1 week to be packed and ready , i said yes ,I stopped my life at that moment ,
everything i had planned and ready to achieved , and jump to the opportunity 5 days later i was on a plane (for the first time) ready for adventure and what an adventure it was , working in a boat has been a life changing experience , after visiting more than 50 countries you stop counting , you met interesting people from all around the world , and there while in Venice Italy i found "Love" my now wife , with who i have 2 wonderful daughters ,when
 you are there on the cruise you live
and eat in a moving city , you save money , money that you can build dreams with , when i was in my country i was living
in Apartment buildings and saw how the landlord was easily collecting money and not being a nice person, so i said i could be

the one collecting the money BUT being a nice person .. so i did ... now i am the Landlord, have my own business ...

Lidiia - RUSSIA

I was 27 years old when I first went on the cruise liner. I would like to start my story about the ship's experience from the very beginning. The idea of such a job arose a couple of years earlier, but my uncertain knowledge of English and fear that it was unrealistic did not allow me to take a step forward. It was an unattainable dream as it seemed to me at that moment. After taking English courses and thoroughly researching ship experience using the all-powerful Internet, I thought that if I didn't do it now I would regret it for the rest of my life. I applied to the one and only agency in my country engaged in employment for cruise ships. After some time, I had an interview with an agency representative, then successfully with a representative of the cruise company. A couple of weeks later, they sent me a letter of employment. Then I started collecting a large number of documents. It was harder than I expected. I was supposed to join in 4 months after the interview, but the company changed it 1 month earlier. It wasn't in my plans of course but I was still happy. After three months and a long flight, I found myself in the land of my childhood dreams, in the United States of America. I was very excited. And then an amazing priceless experience on the great cruise liner was waiting for me. Unforgettable emotions overflowed my soul. This was really what I wanted all my life but I couldn't quite comprehend it. To say that the ship's experience is just a job is nothing to say. It's an incredible life that divides your life into before and after the ship. Moreover this is a harsh school of life in which you learn to kill your fears and build your confidence and organization. These are fun trips to places that you didn't even know about. This is a reality you can't believe.

Unconditionally when I came to the ship, first of all I came to work and earn money. Strict discipline and flexible time management mean high level of responsibility and demand. Working on a ship involves working seven days a week only with breaks for rest and sleep. And this is within a many months. My position is assistant waitress. Despite of having a decent experience as a waiter at home, I would never have thought that a assistant waiter is a individual profession that has particular duties. It is physically very hard. Emotionally, too. But I'm able to handle with emotions but physical pain is more tough. It's better not to get sick on a ship. I think it's better to be physically prepared otherwise you can fall apart and go home. The company provides you with free accomodation and food. I have to pay for all other your needs. My schedule changes every cruise. I can work lunch for one week and I get a good night's sleep. One week I can work breakfast and I have to get up very early but there is an advantage of free time. Or I can work a double shift when I have to go out for both breakfast and lunch but I have short shifts with short breaks. What didn't change every week was the dinner schedule. Every single day I have to prepare my station and come to very big dining room to help my waiter. It would seem nothing complicated. But all that I feel, endure and go through on the ship can not be expressed in words. Due to this experience I have made many friends from all over the world and I have visited amazing places on our planet. And definitely I've become stronger and more confident and I've acquired myself.

Ann– Belgium- Costa Rica

Since I was 10 years old, I wanted to join the police force in Belgium. At 18, I went through the selections exams but didn't pass. My dream crashed, What now? I went to live on my own and went to work in a Restaurant full time. This was in 1999, no smartphones yet, so I was reading the newspaper back then and I found a advertisement about a info night about cruise jobs.

So I went to that info night and got very enthusiastic and made a cv ready to send out to International services (cruise agency in Paris that hired Europeans for cruise jobs) . Some time later I got an invitation to go to Paris for a job interview. Little did I know I was going to be interviewed by the cruise line itself. And right on the spot they said, "you are hired", but we do not have the right date yet for you to get on board since it's a new ship of the company and still under construction in Italy.

But all excited I went back home, made some changes at work and living, and got everything ready. 3 months later I left Belgium and went on a new 4 months (so I thought) adventure…. First to Venice, Italy!

Like I said before it was a new ship, so on arrival we stayed on 2 smaller ships from a Greek cruise line. I applied for dining room, and got a quick service attendants position (later I realized, I should have gotten an assistant server position instead). Quick service is also part of the dining room but you work in a self-service area so no tips, you get a fixed monthly pay. For European norms, not the best pay comparing the hours of work, but I was so happy to be in Italy and on this adventure so in the beginning it didn't matter.

Being part of the dining room we went on board the big ship on a daily basis to clean the dust, to receive the plates and utensils etc… hard work, but so much fun. I was the only Belgian girl and working with more than 50 different nationalities.

After work we where aloud to explore Venice…. Great times.

My roommate at the time was a girl from Costa Rica, so I hanged out with her and she introduced me to the other Costa Ricans that where on board. And one of them caught my eye...

Yep, first day, first contract, first love and guess what? We are still together!

But let me get back first to the work experience first. After a few months in Italy cleaning and getting the ship ready, we were ready for the inaugural sale. With only crew and reporters on board we were getting training, rotations in dining rooms etc. I even spend that time in a guest room, because more crew than crew cabins on board!!

Close to reach my supposedly 4 months contract, they asked me if I could stay another 4 months but being promoted to an assistant server! First I was shocked about the extra time, but than very happy to got promoted, so of course I accepted it. Plus I got to be on the millennium cruise. Partying into the year 2000!

Remember with working on a cruise, you do not get a day off, but time off. So on those days you are aloud to leave the ship in case we were in a port, on sea days we went to a crew pool that was on board for us.

So after the 8 months went back to Belgium, left crying because I had to leave my boyfriend behind...

After 3 months I went to Costa Rica to see him (stayed 3 months) and than a couple of months later, he came to Belgium and there we decided to go back on the cruise to be able to be together and work ... but this time we went to another cruise line. We did 2 contracts on that one, worked in dining room and I also got promoted to be a shipboard trainer. That meant I was in charge of receiving and training the new crew and got a white (officer) uniform and I was free to walk in de guests areas. Loved it!!!

After those 2 contracts it was time to go back to the first company!! With all the experience that I had, I became a dining room server soon and I even became a server at the fine dining restaurant on deck 10, with this incredible view of the ocean!!!

And almost at the end of the 5th contract I was proposed and said Yes! August 2003 I finished my to be last contract, November 2003 went to Costa Rica, January 2004 got married….. By 2008 we had 2 daughters and now 2020 already 16 years married.

So I can say ship life turned my life around!

This was a few real life stories how the work in hospitality can turn the lifes for different, better. So many people got experiences they never thought about, moved to places they dreamed of, doing the jobs where can use all experiences and knowledge. Hospitality is great opportunity. To improve yourself, your business, your LIFE…..

What to say at the end?

Big THANK YOU!

I really thank you from the heart for reading this. I believe that when you are here, you have all the practical information you have learned over time already in practice. All about how to improve yourself, your work, your business.

When I started in this area years ago, there was not much informations available. It's a little better today. If there is something that interests you, you have questions or want to leave me a note I am here for you.

Tell me how this eBook helped you, and what results you got from these tips, what can be improved or done differently.
If you need advice or consultation, please feel free to contact me.

I am looking forward to your emails.

Please write me to linda@worldoflinda.sk

With all best wishes,

Linda Zambrano Dachova

www.ingramcontent.com/pod-product-compliance
Lightning Source LLC
Chambersburg PA
CBHW070459220526
45466CB00004B/1895